CRAFTY
IDEAS FROM
NATURE

Published in Great Britain in 1989 by
**Exley Publications Ltd, 16 Chalk Hill,
Watford, Herts WD1 4BN, United Kingdom.**

Text copyright © Myrna Daitz and the Estate of
the late Shirley Williams, 1989
Illustrations copyright © Gillian Chapman, 1989
Reprinted 1990

British Library Cataloguing in Publication Data
Daitz, Myrna.
   Crafty ideas from nature.
   1. Handicrafts – Manuals.
   I. Title.
   II. Williams, Shirley *1931-1987.*
   745. 5

ISBN 1-85015-171-7

Series designers: Gillian Chapman and
    Linda Sullivan.
Editorial: Margaret Montgomery.
Typeset by Brush Off Studios, St Albans,
    Herts AL3 4PH.
Printed and bound in Hungary.

CRAFTY
IDEAS FROM
NATURE

Myrna Daitz & Shirley Williams

Pictures
by
Gillian Chapman

EXLEY

In the same series, publishing Spring 1990:
Crafty Ideas from Junk
Crafty Ideas for Presents

Publishing Autumn 1990:
Crafty Ideas for Parties

Contents

Introduction

*"Learning by doing"
— and having fun at
the same time!*

Crafty Ideas from Nature contains over forty fun projects for young children of five to eight years. All of the material is drawn from the world of nature around us.

There are plans for growing a miniature garden, for decorating eggs, and for leaf and potato printing. There are ideas for "painting" with different shades of grains of sand, for decorating small boxes with sea shells, and for experimenting with the way different beans and seeds grow. Every step along the way is clearly illustrated and the instructions are so simple that children can follow them on their own, with only minimal help from adults.

Although the projects are fun in themselves, they also provide a lot of educational benefits, teaching manual dexterity and encouraging children to work things out on their own.

The book was authored by Myrna Daitz and Shirley Williams, both themselves parents and school teachers. The illustrator, Gillian Chapman, is the illustrator of several top-selling, early-learning books.

All the projects have been tested by the ultimate consumers – parents and teachers of children in the first years at school.

Each project is designed to give parents the chance to introduce children to the beauty of nature, as they collect material for the projects on family walks.

The authors have only one special request – that is that parents and children take care to ensure that nothing wild is removed and that nature is not destroyed. Special care should be taken in the projects using flowers and bark.

So – we hope you enjoy the book, and have lots of fun!

Your Own Bottle Garden

Parent's Handy Hints:—
Some plants which will do well in the bottle garden are:—
Begonia, Asparagus Fern, Lady Fern, Slow growing Ivy.

What you need :—
A large glass balloon-shaped bottle with a tightly fitting cork.
A handful of small washed pebbles.
A narrow cardboard tube.
A packet of sterilized compost.
1 old fork & 1 old spoon.
2 long sticks.   Adhesive tape.
Watering can with long spout.
A selection of slow growing plants.

1. Lay the bottle on its side and carefully put a layer of small washed pebbles at the bottom.

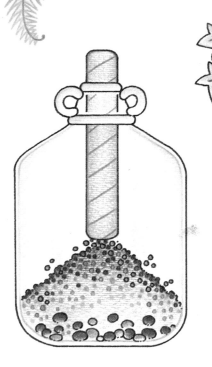

2. Stand the bottle upright and using the cardboard roll as a funnel (to avoid the sides of the bottle) pour in the compost making a layer about 8cm to 10cm (3¼"-4") deep.

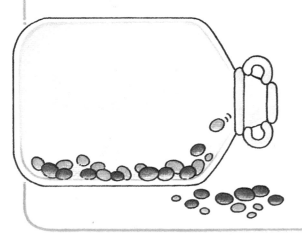

3. Attach the fork and the spoon to the long sticks with adhesive tape so the tools are long enough to reach inside the bottle.

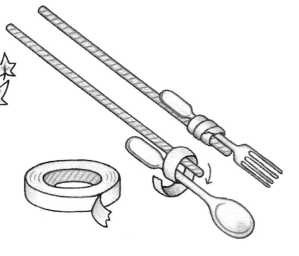

4. Using the tools, place the plants carefully in the bottle and press them down firmly.

5. Water thoroughly and put the cork in tightly. Keep in a light place but <u>not</u> in direct sunlight.

6. Your bottle garden will not need watering for many months.

A Miniature Garden

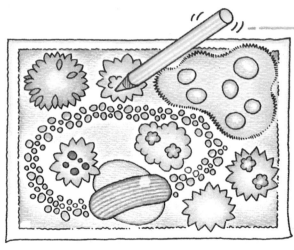

What you need :—
I large plastic seed tray with drainage holes.
I packet of good compost. Gravel.
Several pebbles.
A small mirror.
Small pieces of moss.
A large baking pan.
A selection of small plants, including a miniature Rose.
A piece of tree bark (shed from a tree).

Before you start, draw a plan of your garden on paper, deciding where to put your plants, pool, bridge, path and rock garden. Plan the flowers to make the garden look attractive.

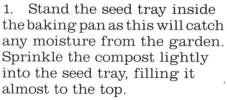

1. Stand the seed tray inside the baking pan as this will catch any moisture from the garden. Sprinkle the compost lightly into the seed tray, filling it almost to the top.

2. To make the rockery, place the moss in one corner of your garden and arrange the stones on and around it.

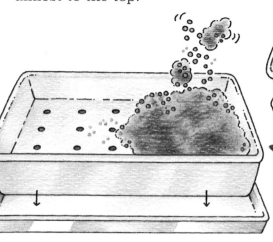

Make sure your child does not press the compost down too firmly, as plants grow better when compost is loosely packed.

3. Plant the miniature rose at the opposite side, firmly pressing in the roots to secure it.

4. Put the mirror in the place you have chosen for the pool and put the bark bridge into position over it. Make a small path using the gravel. To complete your garden, place the plants firmly in the soil.

5. Sprinkle water all over the garden and remember to water once a week.

Parent's Handy Hints :— When the mini garden dies off, the rose and any perennials may be planted outside. Here are some suggestions for plants for your garden — Miniature roses, Campanula (white or blue), Aubretia (purple), Dianthus (pink), Geum (golden), Primula (many shades).

Candy Cone

1. Make sure your cone is perfectly clean and dry.

2. Roll the clay in your hands to warm and soften it, then press it firmly into the middle of the dish.

3. Gently press the cone into the clay in the dish, until it stands very firmly.

4. Starting from the bottom of the cone, place a chocolate button inside each scale. Making sure that you fill them all, work your way slowly up to the top. You will find that the buttons fit inside the scales perfectly.

5. Press the fluffy chicken into the clay and fill the dish with the miniature Easter eggs, completely surrounding the base of the cone. Store in a very cool place until needed.

Parent's Handy Hints :−
This is a perfect gift for Birthdays. It also makes an attractive Easter table decoration. By replacing the chick & eggs with a small Santa and nuts, you can make a Christmas table decoration.

Egg Shell Mosaic

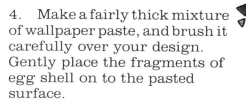

What you need :—
The broken up shells of 6 eggs.
A piece of stiff cardboard.
Bright adhesive tape.
An adhesive picture hook.
Wallpaper paste.
A glue brush.   Scissors.
Drawing paper.   Pencil.
Poster paints and paint
          brush.

Parent's Handy Hints :—
Whenever you use eggs, wash and dry the discarded shells, and use for craft work. If clean & dry the shells will keep indefinitely.

1. Cut the cardboard to the size you require for your picture. Carefully put adhesive tape around the edge of the cardboard to make an attractive border for your mosaic.

2. Plan your design on a piece of paper, and then very carefully draw it on your cardboard. A large bold picture is very attractive.

3. Leave your egg shells in as large pieces as possible to paint. Then when dry, break into small pieces for your mosaic.

4. Make a fairly thick mixture of wallpaper paste, and brush it carefully over your design. Gently place the fragments of egg shell on to the pasted surface.

5. When the picture is completely dry, secure the picture hook to the back.

Sparkling Eggs

Show your child how to bring the eggs slowly to the boil, and then simmer on a very low heat.

What you need :—
An egg, boiled for 20 mins. (and cooled.)
Scissors.
An egg cup.
Glue.
A paste brush.
Tubes of green & yellow glitter (anything bright will do!)
Decorated adhesive tape.

1.   Cut a piece of decorated adhesive tape to fit exactly around the middle of the egg. Press it carefully around the egg.

2.   Brush the top half of the egg with glue and then sprinkle with the first colour of glitter. Stand the egg in an egg cup until the decorated half is dry.

3.   Decorate the bottom half of the egg with your second colour of glitter in exactly the same way. Leave to dry.

These eggs make attractive table decorations for all festive occasions.

16

Mottled Eggs

Parent's Handy Hint:— This only works on white eggs, as the eggs will turn yellow and brown.

What you need :—
An egg, boiled for 20 mins. (and cooled.)
A large, dark skinned onion.
String.
A small piece of muslin.
A saucepan.   Knife.
Cold water.
Spoon.

Help will be needed to peel the onion.

1. Peel the dark skin from the onion. Slightly dampen the skin with warm water.

2.   Wrap the egg firmly in the onion skin, using up all the skin. Wrap the egg in the small piece of muslin and tie it tightly with the string.

3.   Place the egg in the pan, cover with cold water and bring the water slowly to the boil. Turn the heat down very low, and let the water simmer for 25 minutes. Be sure there is enough water in the pan to completely cover the egg and keep checking to see that it has not boiled away.

4.   Remove the egg with a spoon, and leave to cool. Then remove the string, muslin and onion skin. You will now have a mottled golden yellow and brown egg.

Bird's Nest Cakes

What you need:—
8 paper cake cases.
½ coconut (removed from shell).
200g. (7oz.) cooking chocolate.
A saucepan half-filled with hot water.

50g. (2oz.) ground almonds.
50g. (2oz.) confectioner's/ icing sugar.
1 teaspoon lemon juice.
25g. (1oz.) raisins.
1 egg yolk. A wooden spoon.
A grater. A knife.
Heatproof dish.

These Bird's Nests are just right for parties!

Parent's Handy Hint:— Supervision of the melting of the chocolate is advised.

1. Grate the coconut. Put the heatproof dish over the pan of simmering water, break the chocolate into small pieces and let it melt in the dish over the water.

2. When all the chocolate has melted, carefully remove the heatproof dish and using the wooden spoon and the knife spread a thick layer of chocolate in each cake case following the complete shape of the bottom and sides. Let this set for about 10 minutes then give the cake cases a second coating (you may have to put the chocolate in the dish back on the pan of hot water). Put the chocolate coated cases in a cool place to set, then gently peel away the paper leaving a chocolate case.

3. Mix the grated coconut and raisins with the rest of the melted chocolate and fill the chocolate "nests" with the mixture.

4. To make the bird's eggs: Put the almonds, icing sugar, lemon juice and egg yolk in a bowl and knead together well. Shape into eggs, roll in icing sugar and place the "eggs" in the "nests".

Fresh Lemonade

Supervise boiling the water.

What you need :—
3 fresh lemons.
1.5 litres (60 fl.oz.) of cold water.
2 tablespoons of brown sugar.
1 saucepan.
A potato peeler.

A lemon squeezer.
A strainer.
A knife.
A long handled wooden spoon.
A large heat proof bowl.

Parent's Handy Hint :—
Show your child how to use the potato peeler, as this will remove the lemon rind not the pith.

1.   Thoroughly rinse and dry the lemons, and peel them very thinly using the potato peeler.

2.   Put 250ml (10 fl.oz.) of cold water into the saucepan, add the sugar and the lemon rind and stir well. Bring the mixture slowly to the boil and simmer for 10 minutes, stirring occasionally with a long-handled wooden spoon.

3.   Cut the lemons in half, squeeze out the juice into a large bowl, add the rest of the cold water to the lemon juice in the bowl and then very carefully add the hot liquid from the pan and stir well.

4.   When the lemonade is cold, carefully pour it through the strainer into a jug. Add ice cubes and serve.

Leaf Printing

What you need:–
Sheets of white paper or cardboard.
Powder paints.
Paint brushes.
Newspaper.
An assortment of fresh leaves.
Bright adhesive tape.
Adhesive picture hook.

Parent's Handy Hints :–
Make sure all surfaces are covered with newspapers as this is a messy project.
If accidents occur powder paints wash out easily.

1. Mix the paint to a fairly thick consistency and brush it on to the veined underside of the leaf.

2. Place the painted side of the leaf on to the paper or cardboard. Place the newspaper over the leaf and carefully rub.

3. Remove the newspaper and you will have a perfect imprint of the leaf.

4. Repeat this process with different shades of paint and different shaped leaves, building up an attractive picture.

5. Bright adhesive tape can be placed all around the picture to make a decorative frame. Place an adhesive picture hook at the back, and display your leaf print picture.

Potato Printing

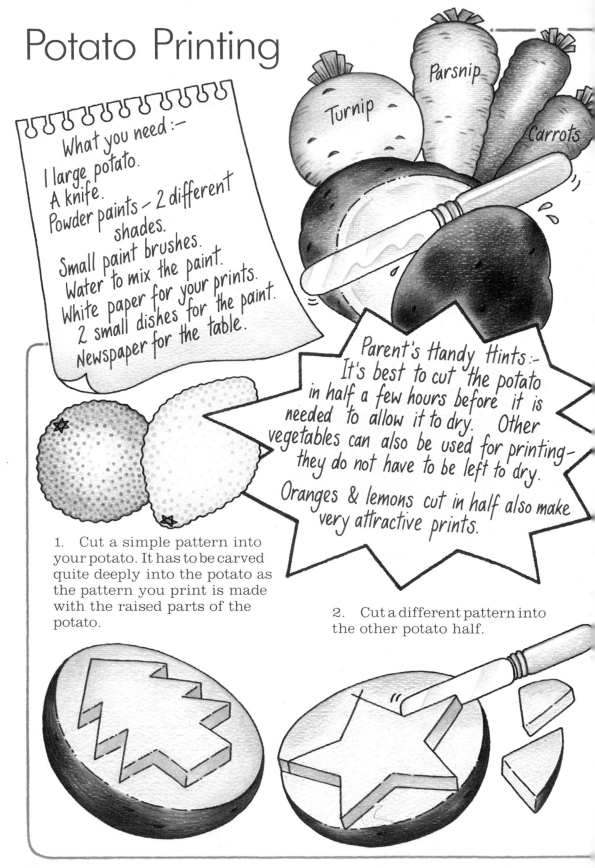

What you need :-
1 large potato.
A knife.
Powder paints – 2 different shades.
Small paint brushes.
Water to mix the paint.
White paper for your prints.
2 small dishes for the paint.
Newspaper for the table.

Turnip

Parsnip

Carrots

Parent's Handy Hints :-
It's best to cut the potato in half a few hours before it is needed to allow it to dry. Other vegetables can also be used for printing – they do not have to be left to dry.

Oranges & lemons cut in half also make very attractive prints.

1. Cut a simple pattern into your potato. It has to be carved quite deeply into the potato as the pattern you print is made with the raised parts of the potato.

2. Cut a different pattern into the other potato half.

3. Mix the paints to a thick consistency. Using the paintbrush, paint the potato blocks.

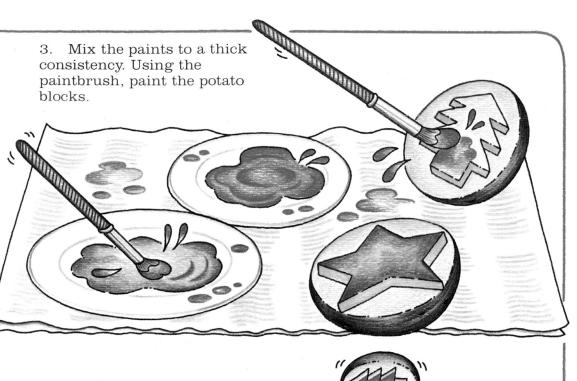

4. Press the potatoes down well on your sheet of white paper. When you have got used to printing in this way, you can start making up interesting designs.
You can print this way on an old tee shirt, but do get permission first.

Seed and Sow

What you need:—
Several large glass jars.
Absorbent paper.
Water.
Bean, pea and radish seeds.

Parent's Handy Hints:—
This is a good project for small children as they can actually watch the seeds growing. Bean sprouts also grow well and are fun to eat. Peanuts grow quickly, but plant the nuts in compost.

1. Line a large jar with absorbent paper and pour in 150ml (5 fl.oz.) water, slightly dampening the paper as you pour the water in.

2. Put the seeds in between the paper and the glass, allowing the paper to hold the seeds. Put three or four of the same kind of seeds in each jar.

3. Keep the jars in a light, warm place and sprinkle with water when the paper feels dry.

4. When your seeds have grown very strong roots, they can be planted out in the spring or summer.

Peas

Beans

Hairy Harry
The Potato Man

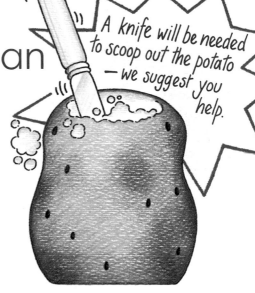

A knife will be needed to scoop out the potato — we suggest you help.

What you need :—
1 very large potato.
Tissues.   Knife.
A packet of cress seeds.
A plastic plant saucer.
A piece of carrot and turnip.
A radish.   Water.
2 toothpicks or used matchsticks.

1.   Cut out a hollow about 3cm (1¼″) deep, according to the size of your potato. Cut a slice off the bottom of the potato so that it will stand up straight.

2.   Cut two small round pieces of carrot to make Harry's eyes, shape a small piece of radish for his nose, cut a mouth from a piece of turnip and, with the edge of a knife, make small slits to look like teeth. Break the toothpicks into small pieces and secure the eyes, nose and mouth to the potato face.

3.   To make Harry's hair, fill the hollow with wet tissues and sprinkle plenty of cress seeds on to it. Pour some water into the plant saucer and stand Harry into it. After a few days, Harry's "hair" will be long enough to cut, wash and eat.

Sand Painting

3. Draw a design on the card and then brush over the design with a thick layer of paste. Sprinkle the sand gently over all the pasted area. Carefully

What you need :—

Silver sand.
Pieces of white cardboard.
Wallpaper paste.
A paste brush.
Powder paint.
Bright adhesive tape.
Pencil.

shake off any surplus sand. Leave the picture to dry for several hours.

1. Cut the cardboard to the size you want your picture to be. Put adhesive tape all round the edges to make a frame for your picture.

2. Gently mix the sand with the powder paint until you have the shade you want.

Parent's Handy Hints :—
Silver sand can be bought at pet stores.
Tiny pieces of stones (used for aquariums) can be used instead of sand.

Showing Your Shells

What you need:−
6 large match boxes.
Paint and paint brush.
Strong glue.
A selection of sea shells.
Tissues.
A saucepan of water.
Absorbent paper.
Cardboard (for labels).
Pencil.

1. Remove the covers of the matchboxes and glue the sides of the bases together to make six separate compartments.

2. Paint the inside and the outer edges of the boxes and leave overnight to dry. When completely dry line each box with tissues.

3. To clean the shells, put them into a pan of cold water and slowly bring it to the boil. Let it boil gently for 4 minutes. Make sure the pan does not boil dry.

Parent's Handy Hints :−
Supervise the sterilizing of the shells.   Open a window when the glue is being used. Help your child identify and label the collection using library books.

4. Leave the shells to drain on absorbent paper until they are perfectly dry.

5. Sort the shells into different shapes, sizes and types and put each different group into your display boxes.

6. Write the names of each different kind of shell on a small piece of card, and place each one in the appropriate box.

Cockles Scallops
Limpets Oysters
Whelks Winkles

Shell Box
of Delights

What you need :-
1 very large matchbox.
A piece of felt.
Small packet of plaster.
An assortment of tiny shells.

Old knife.
Rubber based adhesive.
A small tin of clear varnish
and a brush.

1.   Place the matchbox on the felt, draw around it, and cut out the felt so that it fits the underneath of the matchbox perfectly. Using a rubber-based adhesive, glue the felt to the base of the matchbox.

2.   Remove the inside drawer of the matchbox. Measure the inside of the drawer. Cut and glue another piece of felt to line the drawer.

3.   Mix the plaster into a thick mixture. Coat the top and sides of the matchbox with the mixture, using just enough to hold the shells.

4.   Gently press the shells into the plaster and leave them for several days to dry and harden.

5.   When the box is completely dry, paint the entire surface with clear varnish. Leave to dry, then replace the drawer of the matchbox.

This makes a useful present.

Sea-side Plaque

Parent's Handy Hints :—
Let your child collect shells at the seaside for making shell projects.
If this is not possible then packets of shells can be bought at craft shops.

What you need:—
An old round dinner plate (a thick earthenware one is best.)
An assortment of tiny shells.
A small packet of plaster.
An old mixing bowl, an old spoon and knife.
A strong adhesive picture hook.
+ brush.

1. Mix the plaster in the bowl, making it up to a thick consistency by using twice as much plaster as water.

2. Using the knife, put the plaster on to the plate spreading it about 0.5cm (¼″) thick all over.

3. Starting from the outside edge, gently press the shells into the mixture. Do not press too hard or the shells wsll sink into it. Continue making your design of shells until the whole surface is covered. A large shell in the middle surrounded by tiny shells looks very attractive. Leave the plate on a flat surface for 5 days to completely harden. Firmly secure the picture hook at the back to finish the plaque. Paint all over using a clear varnish.

Open windows when using varnish or glues!

29

Pressed Flowers

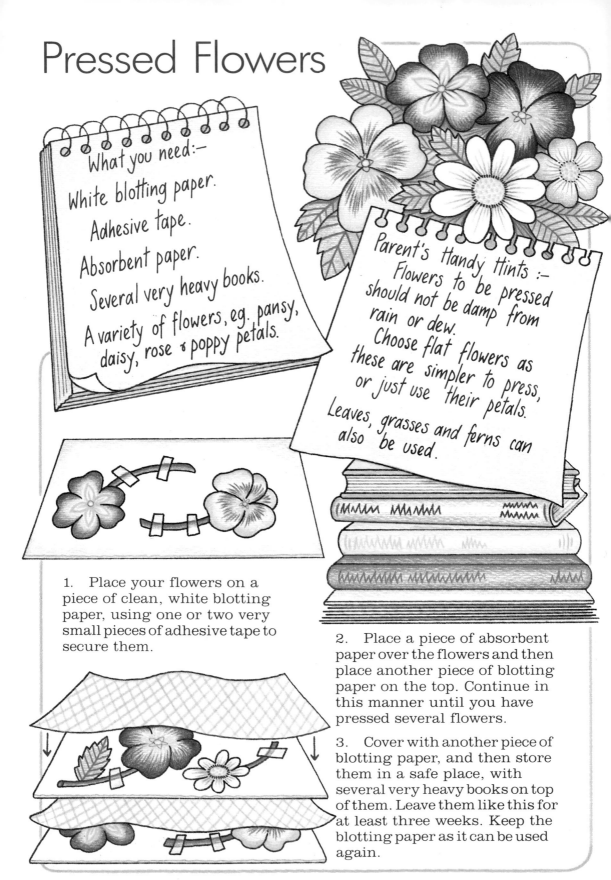

What you need:-
White blotting paper.
Adhesive tape.
Absorbent paper.
Several very heavy books.
A variety of flowers, eg. pansy, daisy, rose & poppy petals.

Parent's Handy Hints :-
Flowers to be pressed should not be damp from rain or dew.
Choose flat flowers as these are simpler to press, or just use their petals.
Leaves, grasses and ferns can also be used.

1. Place your flowers on a piece of clean, white blotting paper, using one or two very small pieces of adhesive tape to secure them.

2. Place a piece of absorbent paper over the flowers and then place another piece of blotting paper on the top. Continue in this manner until you have pressed several flowers.

3. Cover with another piece of blotting paper, and then store them in a safe place, with several very heavy books on top of them. Leave them like this for at least three weeks. Keep the blotting paper as it can be used again.

Pansy Picture

What you need :—
A photograph frame with glass.
A piece of dark blue or
red velvet.
Several pressed pansies & leaves.
Adhesive.   Paste brush.
Pinking shears.
     Pencil.   Ruler.

1. Using the pinking shears, cut the velvet to fit exactly inside the frame so that when it is in place the backing of the frame does not show.

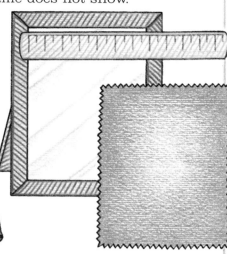

2. Arrange your dried flowers in an attractive pattern on the velvet. When you have decided on the correct positions, put a small amount of the adhesive on the back of each flower and press very gently on to the velvet. Leave the picture to dry for an hour.

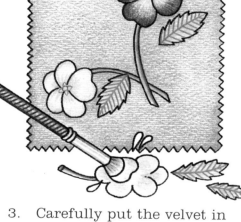

3. Carefully put the velvet in the frame, taking care not to knock the flowers. The glass should press very tightly on to the flowers.

Parent's Handy Hint :—
Non-reflective glass in the frame makes the picture even more attractive.

Floral Notepaper

What you need :-
Pressed flowers (see p.30).
Transparent book covering with adhesive backing.
Plain notepaper with envelopes.
Small flat boxes or trays used by supermarkets to pack fruit and cans.
Tweezers.
Ruler.
Scissors.
Film.

Parent's Handy Hints :-
Pressed flowers can be used to decorate greetings cards, book marks, gift tags, place cards, trays, lamp shades and waste paper baskets.

All the flowers on these items <u>must</u> be covered with transparent book covering with adhesive backing as they are dry and brittle and easily damaged.

1. Using tweezers, gently lay a few flowers on the top of your sheet of notepaper. Carefully move them around until you are satisfied with your design.

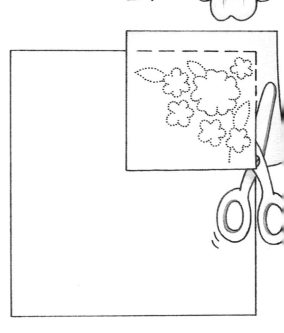

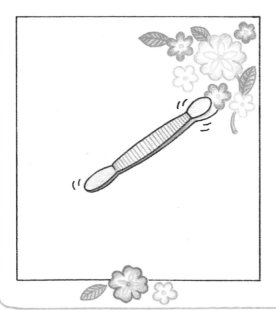

2. Cut small squares of the transparent paper just large enough to completely cover your flower design.

3. Peel the backing from the transparent paper and lay the paper sticky side up flat on the table.

4. One by one, transfer the flowers to the sticky paper and place them face down so that you will see the <u>front</u> of the flowers when you turn the paper over. Press the flowers gently on to the adhesive until they are secure.

If you make a large collection of dried flowers during the summer, they can be stored between sheets of paper to use later.

5. Taking great care, turn the transparent paper over and press it firmly on to your notepaper. Smooth over gently to remove any air bubbles.

6. When all the sheets of notepaper have been decorated, place them with the envelopes in the boxes and cover the tray with cling film. This makes a delightful gift for special occasions.

Lavender Cat on a Cushion

1. Take 2 pieces of cotton material 5cm wide x 10cm long (2" x 4") to make the cushion.

2. With the right sides together, sew round the material leaving 2cm (¾") open. Turn it the right side out.

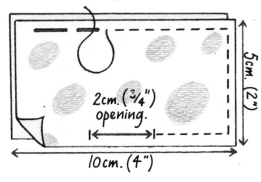

2cm. (¾") opening.

5cm. (2")

10cm. (4")

What you need :—
Cotton material for the cushion. Scissors.
Nylon fur.
Needle and cotton.
Dried lavender flowers.*
2 toy's safety eyes.*
(* both available from craft shops)
Kapok or old pantyhose (for stuffing.)

6. Sew the 2 cat shapes together, this time over sewing them and keeping both shapes the right side out. Again leave 2cm (¾") unstitched. The cat must then be stuffed with kapok or cut up scraps of pantyhose. Sew up the opening firmly to seal.

7. Join the cat to the cushion by sewing the two together so that the cat sits on the cushion.

3. Stuff the cushion with dried lavender flowers through the opening and sew it up firmly.

4. Cut out a paper pattern of a cat and, using the nylon fur material, cut out two cat shapes.

"I am the PURR-fect present!"

5. Make 2 small holes with the point of your scissors in the head of the cat shape, and press in 2 small eyes which are then safely fixed at the back with clips.

Home Made Perfume

What you need :–
A small glass jar with a tight fitting lid. Water.
An assortment of fresh petals which are highly perfumed – eg. roses and carnations.
An empty perfume bottle.
Ribbon, to make a bow.
Tiny perfume funnel (sold at pharmacies.)

Parent's Handy Hint:–
We recommend you advise your child which flowers you can spare from the flower border!

1. Gather a selection of highly-perfumed, fresh petals.

2. Thoroughly wash and dry the small glass jar. One at a time place the petals in the jar until it is completely full.

3. Fill the bottle with water until it will hold no more, then screw on the lid very tightly. Gently shake the bottle, then leave it to settle. You may have to add a little more water after a few days. Screw the lid back on very tightly and leave it for three to four weeks.

4. Strain and carefully pour the perfume through the funnel into the empty perfume bottle. Tie the ribbon around the bottle and finish with a pretty bow. This makes a delightful gift.

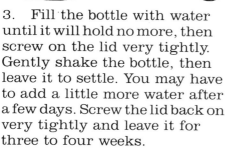

This makes a delightful gift.

Bark Rubbings

1.   Tape the paper to the bark of the tree and rub firmly with a crayon, using the side of the crayon <u>not</u> the point. Take care not to tear the paper.

2.   As you gently, but firmly, rub, you will see the bark pattern appear.

3.   Using a reference book, carefully identify the type of tree, and write its name on your bark rubbing.

4.   When you have a large and varied collection, draw a pretty cover, and staple all the sheets together. You now have an interesting book of bark rubbings.

What you need:—
Sheets of strong white paper, approx. 20x30 cm. (8" x 12").
Assorted wax crayons.
A stapler.
Adhesive tape.

oak

pine

Bark Rubbings

Parent's Handy Hint :—
The easiest way to kill a tree is to strip it's bark !
Use only the bark of dead trees.

Trees From Pips and Stones

What you need :-
Several small plant pots
— with saucers.
The same number of clean
jam jars.
Special seed compost.
Pips — from oranges, lemons,
grapefruit or tangerines. Stones—
peach, date, cherry or apricot.

1. Fill the plant pots with the compost and push two pips OR one stone into the compost until they are covered.

2. Sprinkle with enough water to dampen the compost, then cover each plant pot with an upturned jam jar. This makes a miniature greenhouse.

orange pips   peach stone

3. Leave the pots in a warm, dark place until the pip or stone begins to sprout. Check from time to time that the compost is moist, as the seed could take some weeks to germinate.

4. When the pip or stone begins to sprout, remove the jam jar and put the pot into a light, airy place.

Parent's Handy Hints :—
Help your child to label and date each plant.
Special seed compost is available at gardening shops.
Make sure your child does not over-water the plants.

peach   orange   date   cherry

Pasta Polly Parrot

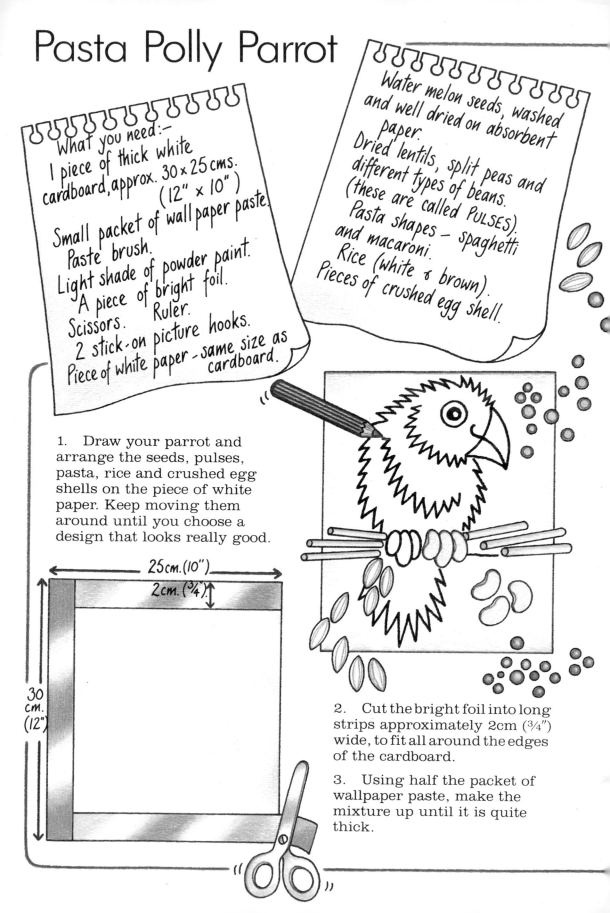

1. Draw your parrot and arrange the seeds, pulses, pasta, rice and crushed egg shells on the piece of white paper. Keep moving them around until you choose a design that looks really good.

25cm.(10")

2cm.(¾")

30 cm. (12")

2. Cut the bright foil into long strips approximately 2cm (¾") wide, to fit all around the edges of the cardboard.

3. Using half the packet of wallpaper paste, make the mixture up until it is quite thick.

4. Add 2 teaspoonfuls of the powder paint, and mix well until it has blended in.

5. Spread the paste all over the cardboard.

6. Stick the foil around the edges of the picture to make a very attractive frame.

7. Following your own design, place your seeds, pulses, rice and crushed egg shells on to the glued surface of the cardboard. Complete one area at a time, pressing gently onto the paste.

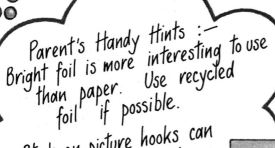

Parent's Handy Hints :—
Bright foil is more interesting to use than paper. Use recycled foil if possible.

Stick-on picture hooks can be bought in most hardware shops.

Water melon seeds keep well when washed and dried thoroughly.

Egg shell should be washed, dried and crushed in between paper.

8. Leave to dry for a couple of days.

9. Attach two picture hooks to the back of your collage, using either adhesive tape or glue.

Feather Headdress

Parent's Handy Hints :—
Seagull feathers are large, so keep a lookout for them if you visit the seaside.
Otherwise feathers can be bought at craft shops.

1.   Fold the card in half lengthways and, keeping the open edge to the top, draw a feather design all the way round the outside of the cardboard. Decorate with felt-tipped pens.

55 cm. (22")

12 cm. (5")

40

Open the card and place on a table, putting the patterned side down.

3. Glue the feather quills firmly along the back of the pattern.

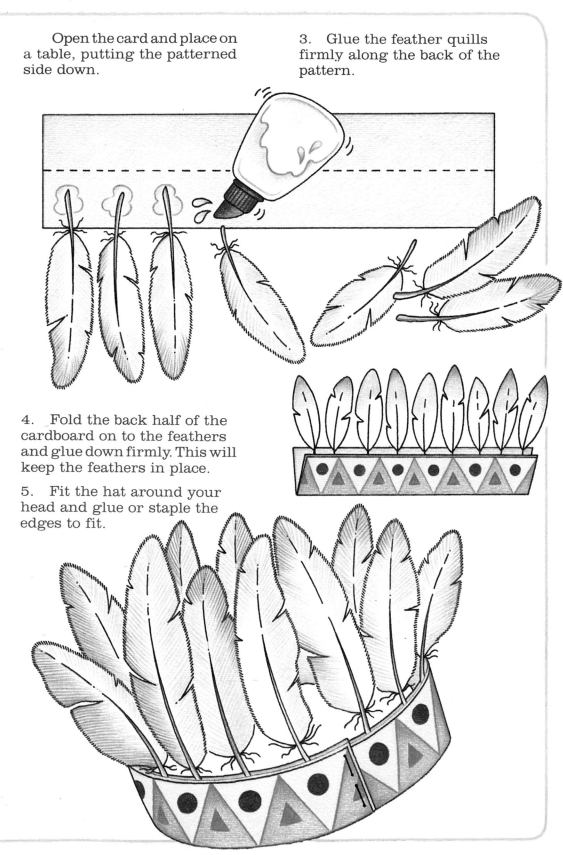

4. Fold the back half of the cardboard on to the feathers and glue down firmly. This will keep the feathers in place.

5. Fit the hat around your head and glue or staple the edges to fit.

Stonecraft Monster

What you need :–
1 large pebble for the body.
1 large pebble for the head.
2 small flat pebbles for the feet.
Scraps of felt.
Clear varnish.
Glue.
Glue brush.

1. Turn the large stone over and put some glue on the two places where you will fix the feet. Put glue on to the two flat pebbles and leave for 5 minutes for the glue to become very tacky, then press the "feet" firmly into position.
Turn the monster over and glue the "head" pebble on in the same way.

2. Paint the monster all over with the clear varnish and leave to dry.

3. Cut the felt to the shape of the head, ears and tail and glue to the monster. Cut out the teeth and eye shapes from the felt and glue in position.

Try making other stonecraft models. If you make a collection of stones and pebbles, look for suitably shaped ones to make animals, birds or people.

Parent's Handy Hints :–
Allow your child to collect pebbles for craft work. Pebbles should be well washed and dried before use.

Painted Stones

What you need :—

Large, very smooth, white stones.
Acrylic paint in several different shades.
A paintbrush.
A rag.
A tin of clear varnish.

Parent's Handy Hints :—

Make sure a window is open when using acrylic paint and varnish.

Does the shape of a stone suggest anything to you ?
A sleeping animal or a face?

Paint some stones with your own ideas !

1. Wash and thoroughly dry your stone.

2. Using the paint quite thickly, cover the stone completely with one shade. Wash and dry your paintbrush and then quickly drop splashes of a different shade of paint over the wet stone. Let the paint run down and mingle with the base coat to give a delightful shaded effect.

3. Cover several stones in this way, using as many different shades of paint as you have. Leave to dry for 2 to 3 hours.

4. Paint all over the stones with a layer of clear varnish. Leave to dry.

If placed together in a pretty dish, these stones look very attractive as a table decoration.

43

Dried Leaf Owl

What you need :—
An assortment of dried leaves.
A piece of white cardboard approx. 20 × 30 cm. (8" × 12")
An adhesive picture hook.
Cellulose glue.   Pencil.
Glue brush.
A large picture of an OWL.

Parent's Handy Hint:—
Use a cellulose glue, as water based glue could make the leaves rot.

1. Dry the leaves in the same way as the method we have given for drying flowers on page 50.

2. Trace a picture of an animal or bird on to the white cardboard, using all the space available.

3. Place the leaves on your drawing, and keep re-arranging them until you have the picture just as you want it.

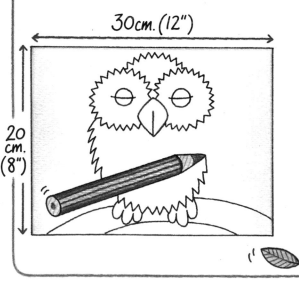

30cm. (12")

20 cm. (8")

4.   One by one glue each leaf on to your picture using different sizes and shapes of leaves to make your picture interesting.

Make sure a window is open when using the cellulose glue!

BACK VIEW

5.   When the picture is completely dry, attach the adhesive picture hook to the back.

Apple Surprises

Supervise the boiling and simmering of the water.

What you need :-

8 small apples.

8 lollipop sticks.

200g. (7oz.) unsweetened cooking chocolate.

100g. (3½oz.) dried banana flakes.

A saucepan half filled with boiling water.

A heatproof basin.

A wooden spoon.

Waxed cooking paper.

Parent's Handy Hint :- Choose apples with a long stalk on them, then these can be bent around the stick to hold the apple firmly.

1. Wash the apples and dry on absorbent paper. Push a stick firmly into each apple and twist the stalk round the stick. Break the chocolate into small pieces and put into a heatproof basin. Place the basin on top of a pan of gently simmering water.

2. When the chocolate is soft and runny, carefully remove the basin from the saucepan and dip each apple into the chocolate. Turn the apple round and round using the stick until the apple is well covered.

3. Lift the apple out carefully and then roll the chocolate apple in a flat dish of flaked banana chips. Stand the apples, with the stick pointing up, on the waxed paper to set. Store in a very cold place or in a refrigerator.

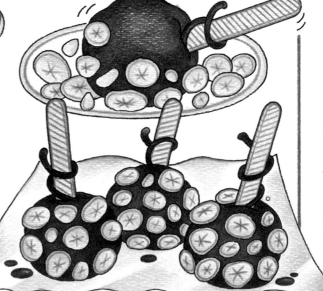

A Halloween Lantern

1. Choose a large turnip or pumpkin that will stand firmly on a flat surface. Cut off a 5cm (2″) piece from the top. Scoop out most of the inside with the sharp knife and the spoon, leaving 2cm (¾″) of flesh all round the inside of the lantern.

2. Carefully cut out the eyes, nose and mouth shapes.

3. Place your candle holder and candle inside the lantern. When you light the candle the light will shine through the eyes, nose and mouth.

Have a very scary Halloween!

Parent's Handy Hint :—
It is safer to have the candle firmly fixed in a saucer-type candle holder.

The Crazy Cucumber

What you need :–
A cucumber.
3 small thin carrots.
A small turnip.
3 small radishes.
A lettuce.

2 tiny button mushrooms.
A flat tray.
Several toothpicks.
A knife.

1. Shred the lettuce and place it on the tray. This is for the Crazy Cucumber to sit on.

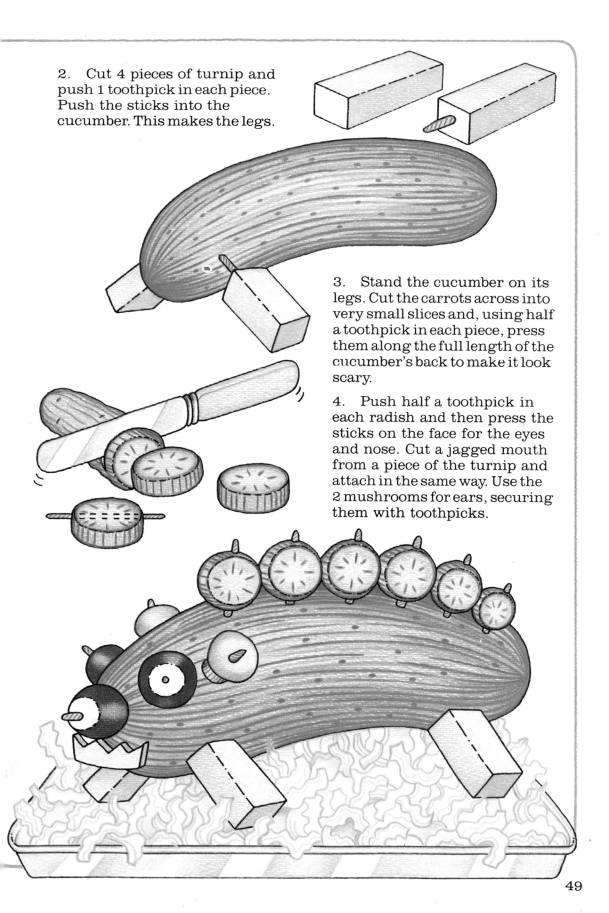

2. Cut 4 pieces of turnip and push 1 toothpick in each piece. Push the sticks into the cucumber. This makes the legs.

3. Stand the cucumber on its legs. Cut the carrots across into very small slices and, using half a toothpick in each piece, press them along the full length of the cucumber's back to make it look scary.

4. Push half a toothpick in each radish and then press the sticks on the face for the eyes and nose. Cut a jagged mouth from a piece of the turnip and attach in the same way. Use the 2 mushrooms for ears, securing them with toothpicks.

Dried Flowers

Parent's Handy Hints :—
Encourage your child to collect flowers, grasses & leaves.
Oasis is available from florists and is the base of flower arrangements.

1. DRYING METHODS. The following plants are hung upside down in bunches and left to dry for a month somewhere warm – mignonette; poppy seed heads; chinese lanterns; hare's tail grass and all other grasses.

Beech nuts are gathered with as much stem as possible and can be left natural or painted with silver or gold paint.

Instructions for glycerined preserved leaves can be found on the opposite page (page 51).

Helichrysum should be picked when the flowers are still tight. Then push a piece of florist's wire up the short stem and stand up to dry in a jar for 2 to 3 weeks.

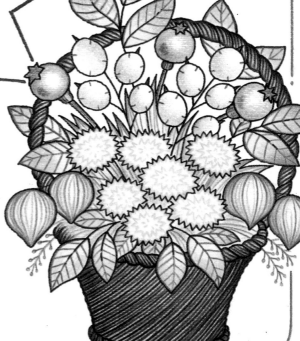

2. Push a piece of oasis firmly into the container and using the glycerined leaves make a basic outline, trimming the stems until you have the size you want.

3. Fill in the shape gradually, using flowers and leaves of the right size and shade to make a beautiful and everlasting arrangement.

Everlasting Leaves

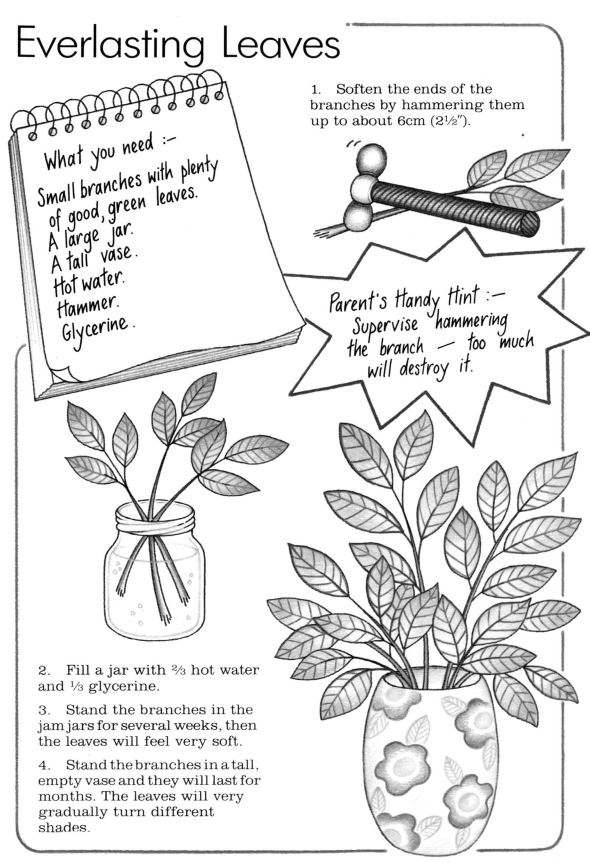

What you need :-
Small branches with plenty of good, green leaves.
A large jar.
A tall vase.
Hot water.
Hammer.
Glycerine.

1. Soften the ends of the branches by hammering them up to about 6cm (2½").

Parent's Handy Hint :-
Supervise hammering the branch — too much will destroy it.

2. Fill a jar with ⅔ hot water and ⅓ glycerine.

3. Stand the branches in the jam jars for several weeks, then the leaves will feel very soft.

4. Stand the branches in a tall, empty vase and they will last for months. The leaves will very gradually turn different shades.

Silver Leaf Jar

1. Cut a piece of foil the right size to fit all around the jar, leaving a small piece to fold over the inside of the top of the jar.

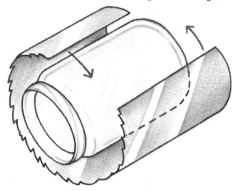

What you need :-
A collection of small fresh leaves.
A jar with a screw top lid.
Adhesive.
A piece of silver foil.
A piece of thin cardboard.
Scissors.
An old, soft toothbrush.

2. Dry your leaves on absorbent paper, then glue them on to the thick cardboard. When dry, carefully cut out the leaf shapes. They will now be much thicker with the cardboard glued to them.

Parent's Handy Hints :-
Make sure your child smoothes out the foil with the ball of the fingers, not with the nails as the foil will tear easily.

3. Glue the leaves on to the jar, covering as much of the jar as possible. Leave to dry.

4. Very gently crush the foil in your hands, then gently smooth it out. This makes it easier to handle. Spread glue all over the dull side of the foil. Carefully press the foil all around the sides of the jar (do not cover the base) and tuck the excess inside the top of the jar. Using a very soft toothbrush, gently tap all the leaves so that their pattern shows through the foil. Cover the lid with silver foil, and screw it on to the jar.

Melon Seed Necklace

1. Wash and thoroughly dry the melon seeds.

2. Cut the button thread to the size you need for your necklace. Tie a knot at one end of the thread.

What you need :—
Melon seeds.
Strong white button thread.
A darning needle.
Poster paints σ brush
Newspapers.   Scissors.

3. Thread the darning needle and very carefully push the needle and thread through each melon seed. String the seeds in this way until the whole length of thread is almost full. Tie the end of the thread to the knot you started with.

4. Spread out the finished necklace on a sheet of newspaper and very carefully paint the seeds. Remove the necklace from the newspaper and hang up to dry. Repeat the painting process on the back of the seeds. Hang up to dry.

Parent's Handy Hints :—
Make sure you put down plenty of newspaper before your child starts painting!

Snowstorm

What you need :-
A small round jar with a tight fitting lid.
Small packet of plaster.
2 or 3 small branched twigs.
1 tablespoon grated coconut.
Plastic cake decoration – eg. a snowman.
1 teaspoon.

Parent's Handy Hint :-
Help your child to mix the plaster to a thick consistency.

1. Make up half of the packet of plaster and spoon it into the bottom of the jar.

2. Just before it starts to set, place your twigs and snowman into the mixture, and press round them with a spoon so that they stand up firmly. Leave overnight to harden and set in the base.

This makes a lovely gift.

3. Add cold water to almost fill the jar and put in 1 tablespoonful of grated coconut.

4. Put the lid on tightly, gently shake the jar and you will have a pretty snowstorm.

A Festive Candle

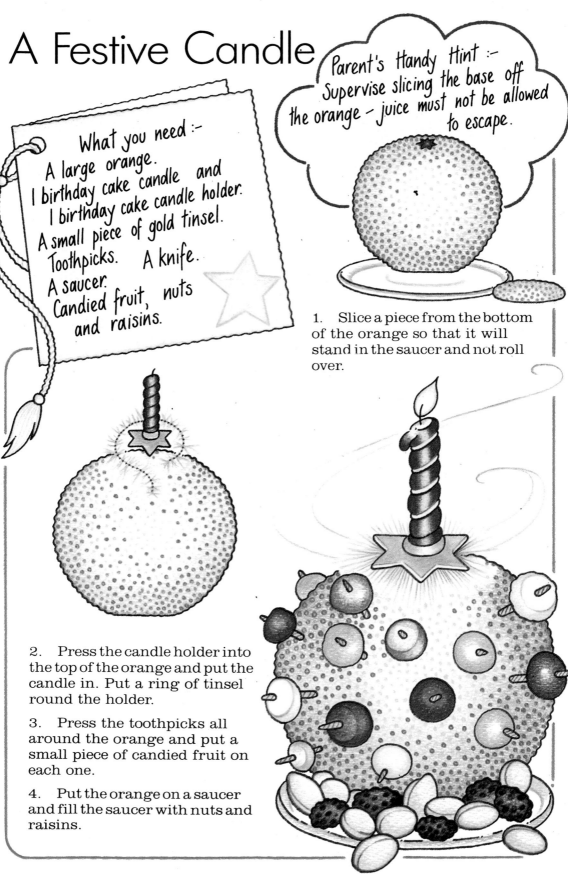

Parent's Handy Hint :- Supervise slicing the base off the orange – juice must not be allowed to escape.

What you need :-
A large orange.
1 birthday cake candle and 1 birthday cake candle holder.
A small piece of gold tinsel.
Toothpicks.   A knife.
A saucer.
Candied fruit, nuts and raisins.

1.   Slice a piece from the bottom of the orange so that it will stand in the saucer and not roll over.

2.   Press the candle holder into the top of the orange and put the candle in. Put a ring of tinsel round the holder.

3.   Press the toothpicks all around the orange and put a small piece of candied fruit on each one.

4.   Put the orange on a saucer and fill the saucer with nuts and raisins.

Little Nut Tree

1. Cover the plant pot with the paper, and secure with adhesive tape.

What you need :—
A 15cm. (6") plant pot.
Wrapping paper.
Adhesive tape.
A selection of nuts, raisins and sweets.   Model clay.
Small fir cones.
An interesting branch with twigs.
A needle and thread.

2. Put a large piece of model clay inside the pot, pressing it firmly to the base and making sure it is in the middle.

3. Press the branch into the model clay to make it stand firmly, then fill the pot up to the top with soil.

4. Wrap nuts and raisins in the paper.

5. Thread the needle. Carefully push the needle and thread through the paper wrapping of the nuts and raisins. Tie lengths of thread around the top of each small fir cone, leaving a loop at the top, and then hang them all from the twigs.

Parent's Handy Hints :—
This makes a delightful table decoration for a party.
Small messages can be slipped inside the wrappings with the nuts and sweets !

A Tree Bauble

What you need :-
A ping-pong ball.
An egg cup.
Felt tipped pens.
Clear varnish
A paint brush.
A very long sewing needle.
Sewing thread.

1. Punch a hole at either end of the ping-pong ball, with the needle.

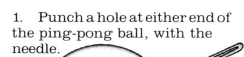

2. Stand the ball in the egg cup. This makes it easier to handle while decorating. Draw your design on the ball with the felt tipped pens. Turn the ball over and stand the decorated end in the egg cup, so that you can decorate the other half.

3. Carefully paint all over the ball with the clear varnish. Leave to completely dry.

4. Thread the needle with the sewing thread. Put the needle through the tiny hole at the top of the ball, and very carefully pull the thread all the way through the ball and out the other end. Remove the needle. Make a tight knot in the thread to secure the ball. Hang the bauble from a branch of a tree.

Parent's Handy Hint :-
These baubles make wonderful Christmas decorations.

Coconut Bird Feeder

What you need :-
I large coconut.
A strong knife. Hammer.
Screwdriver.
A piece of string, approx.
60 cm. (24") long.
100g. (4oz.) white cooking fat.
½ cup of breadcrumbs.
½ cup of cake crumbs.
¼ cup of nuts.
¼ cup of raisins.

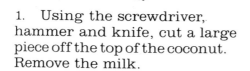

Parent's Handy Hint :-
Supervise the melting
of the cooking fat.

straight when you fill the coconut.

3. To make the filling, slowly melt the cooking fat in a saucepan over a low heat. Fill the coconut shell to the top with the bread crumbs, cake crumbs, nuts and raisins. Make sure that the string is still in an upright position, then pour the hot fat into the shell until it is full. Leave this to get completely cold and solid before you hang the coconut bird feeder outside.

1. Using the screwdriver, hammer and knife, cut a large piece off the top of the coconut. Remove the milk.

2. Using the screwdriver and hammer, make a hole in the middle of the base. Thread the string through the hole, and make a big knot underneath the coconut to secure the string. Hang it up, so that the string is

Peanut Birdmobile

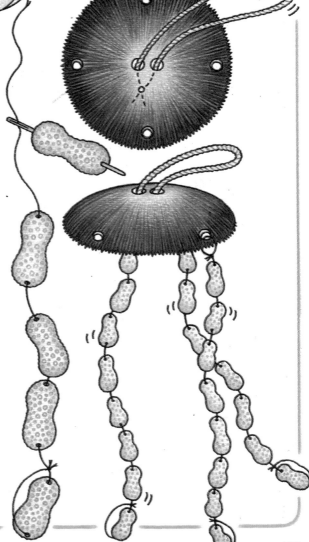

What you need :-
0.5 kg. (1 lb.) unshelled peanuts.
A reel of strong thread.
A darning needle.
60cm. (24") of nylon cord.
½ coconut.
1 large nail.
Hammer.

1. Make 2 holes in the top of the coconut by gently hammering in a nail. Remove the nail. To make the hanger, thread the nylon cord through the holes and tie the ends tightly together inside the coconut.

2. Hammer 4 evenly-spaced holes into the coconut.

3. Cut a length of thread 75cm (30") long and make a string of peanuts by pushing the needle and thread all the way through the first nut, avoiding the small nuts inside. Tie the thread round the first nut only and make a knot to stop the nuts falling off. Carry on threading the nuts until you have 12-15 nuts on the thread. Push the needle and thread through 1 of the 4 holes in the coconut, remove the needle from the thread and tie the thread into a tight knot. Trim off any remaining thread.

4. Repeat this 3 more times, making sure that the 4 strings of nuts are evenly balanced. Hang the coconut from a tree and see how many different kinds of birds you can spot enjoying your birdmobile.

Squirrels
Nutty Game

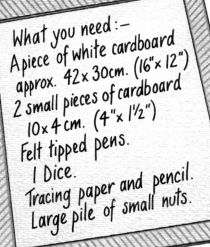

What you need :-
A piece of white cardboard
approx. 42 x 30cm. (16" x 12")
2 small pieces of cardboard
10 x 4 cm. (4" x 1½")
Felt tipped pens.
1 Dice.
Tracing paper and pencil.
Large pile of small nuts.

1. Copy the pattern of the game on to your large piece of cardboard.

2. Carefully write all the instructions in the squares.

3. Decorate the game with a woodland scene.

4. Fold two small pieces of cardboard in half lengthways so that they stand up. These are your moveable squirrel markers.

5. Decorate your markers by either drawing on a squirrel or tracing the one on our game. Make the two markers different, so there is one for each player.

For the
Game Template
see pages 62-63.

Parent's Handy Hints :-
Red peanuts are cheap and nutritious, but nuts shouldn't be given to small children as they can get stuck in their throats.

Rules of the Game
The aim of the game is to help the squirrels find their missing store of nuts.

Take turns to throw the dice, the person to get the highest number goes first. Place your squirrel markers on square 1.

Each person in turn throws the dice, and follows the instructions on the square on which the marker lands.

If you land on a square that demands more nuts than you have won, simply put back whatever you have left.

Keep a large dish of nuts on the table to act as the store.

The winner is the first person to safely reach the last square, which is the squirrel's hoard of nuts. As the reward you can nibble the nuts.

Shuttlecocks

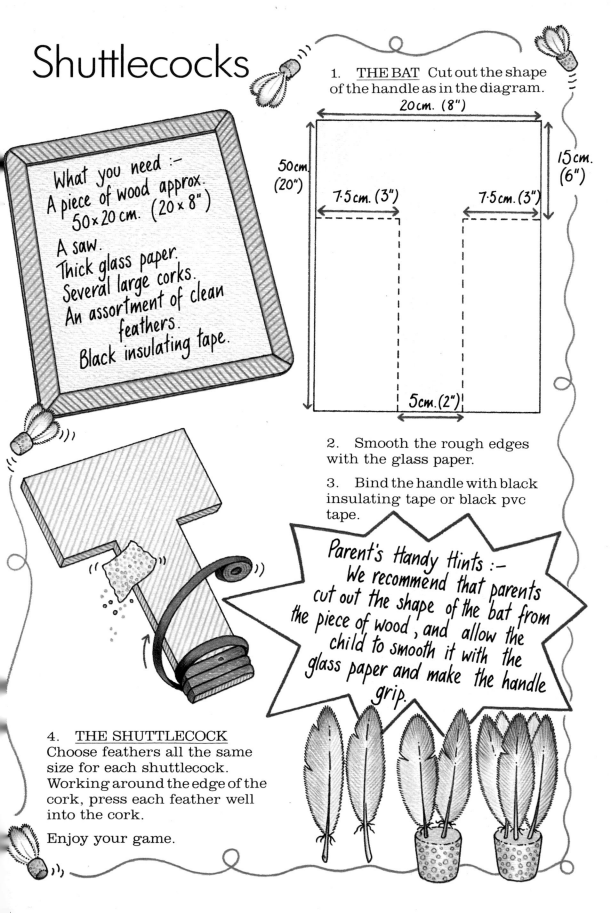

What you need :-
A piece of wood approx. 50 × 20 cm. (20 × 8")

A saw.
Thick glass paper.
Several large corks.
An assortment of clean feathers.
Black insulating tape.

1. THE BAT Cut out the shape of the handle as in the diagram.

20 cm. (8")
50 cm. (20")
15 cm. (6")
7.5 cm. (3")
7.5 cm. (3")
5 cm. (2")

2. Smooth the rough edges with the glass paper.

3. Bind the handle with black insulating tape or black pvc tape.

Parent's Handy Hints :-
We recommend that parents cut out the shape of the bat from the piece of wood, and allow the child to smooth it with the glass paper and make the handle grip.

4. THE SHUTTLECOCK
Choose feathers all the same size for each shuttlecock. Working around the edge of the cork, press each feather well into the cork.

Enjoy your game.

Squirrels Nutty Game

10.

11. You trip over a log and drop 5 nuts.

12

9. A rabbit gives you 3 nuts.

8. Porcupine in sight... Run back 2 spaces!

7. A mean ferret sends you the wrong way. Miss a turn!

6.

5. You find 4 nuts hidden in a hollow tree.

4.

3.

2. Two birds are hiding close by — give them each a nut.

1. START with 10 nuts.